MORE PR

TOM PICKARD

MORE PRICKS THAN PRIZES

2010 | PRESSED WAFER | BOSTON

Thanks to the editors of Square One *where extracts from this work were first published.*

PRESSED WAFER

9 Columbus Square, Boston Massachusetts 02116

Copyright © 2010 by Tom Pickard

ISBN 978-0-9824100-9-7   FIRST EDITION

Printed by Thomson-Shore, Dexter, Michigan

"**D**o you think this hash is coated with opium, Basil?"

Basil Bunting took his lunch break upstairs in the Rose and Crown where he grumbled about having to proof read stocks and shares all morning for the local rag while his eyes were thickening with cataracts. He took the handful of quid deals of the "black Paki" hashish that I was selling around the pubs and held one to his nose and sniffed it, then shook his head in discouragement and suggested that I was taking too many risks for too small a reward. There was a truth in that and I was lucky not to have been caught because each sale was an exposure to the risk of arrest. It made sense to sell larger quantities in fewer transactions. Although I worked the pubs with a couple of friends, The Body Beef and Jock the Fox, and we alternated making the sale in the busy bars with keeping watch by the door and holding the stash, it was still too many risks for

5

too little money. But it fed the kids and paid the rent and mostly kept the bailiffs off our backs. Mostly; a week earlier my typewriter, writing desk and chair had been sequestrated along with a few other domestic items and sold in the auction room at the bottom of the street for pennies.

"Let's have another pint of Bass, Tom." The poet gave me the money and I went to the counter to collect the drinks. When I returned he was taking the first pull on a "full strength" Senior Service cigarette and enjoying it. He took up his drink and after swallowing a mouthful told me of smoking opium with the chief of police in Tehran towards the end of World War II. When I queried his keeping such company he said; "He was an amusing bloke. On one occasion, after a smoke, the charcoal stove flared up and set fire to the curtains."

"Fuckinell," I interjected.

"All we could do was lie back and admire the flames until a servant ran in to extinguish them."

"How'd you come to know him?"

"He used to visit me once or twice a week to compare notes.'

And perhaps anticipating my next question and forestalling it with a direct look in the eye, which somehow forbade and foretold, he began another story.

"Late one dark night an alcoholic, an opium smoker and a hashish smoker arrived outside of the high city walls to find the gates locked until morning. It was very cold, there was no shelter and they were ill-clothed and ill-shod. Let's smash the door down, said the alcoholic. Let's crawl through the keyhole said the hashish smoker. Let's float over the wall said the opium addict."

He handed the quid deals back to me.

"You know, Tom, the best way for a poet to survive, without a patron, is to find a sinecure. It used to be the Church, but these days it's more likely the BBC, or the British Council, or the universities, I suppose. Anyway I've got to get back to bloody work."

As we walked through the Bigg Market lanes towards the newspaper offices at Thompson House he told me that the city centre was built around a medieval street plan. Then, before clocking in, said; "Of course they'd never give you a sinecure, but you might be able to manage in a country where the standard of living is low."

o o o

There are careful calculations, amongst Basil
Bunting's papers, on the cost of surviving in the
Canary Islands in 1933 where he'd gone to live
after finding life in Rapallo intolerable because
of his friend and mentor's alarming enthusiasm
for Mussolini. Bunting wasn't alone in being
repelled by the fascist crowd beginning to sur-
round Ezra Pound; another of Pound's former
disciples hired a plane and dropped anti-fascist
leaflets over Italy until he was shot down and
killed. From Tenerife, in 1934, Bunting wrote
to Pound: "Every anti-Semitism, anti-nigger-
ism, anti-moorism, that I can recall in history
was base, had its foundations in the meanest
kind of envy and in greed. It makes me sick
to see you covering yourself with that kind of
filth. It is not an arguable question, has not been
arguable for at least nineteen centuries . . . it is
hard to see how you are going to stop the rot
of your mind and heart without a pretty thor-
oughgoing repudiation of what you have spent
a lot of work on. You ought to have the courage for that: but I confess I don't expect to see
it." It must have been a difficult letter to write

as Pound had taught him a great deal about poetry up to that moment—and he knew there was a long way to go. His apprenticeship to Pound begun in the early twenties when the older poet, hearing of the young Northumbrian's ballad and musical hall repertoire, got him out of jail after a drunken barney with a Parisian policeman. Bunting liked to recall that the jail stood on the same site as the one that held the 15th century poet François Villon while he composed in the shadow of the gallows.

Life on Tenerife was comfortable, as they had just enough money to employ a maid and live in a decent pension. His American wife, Marion, recalled that "he was frustrated by the hatred the English on the island felt for him . . . that he was almost insane." Marian attended Popular Front meetings while Bunting preferred to play chess on the hotel balcony with whoever would give him a game. He found a companionable partner in the American Carl Derup who confirmed, "he felt ill at ease with colonial types and did not make friends easily, did not meet any English people in all the time he was there. We shared a common bond in our aversion and fear of fascism, and I spent many hours listening to BB interpreting the news."

After February 1936 he found another occasional chess partner. Spain's Republican government had demoted General Francisco Franco and sent him into exile, as governor of the Canaries, where he continued to plot his fascist coup. While Bunting played chess with the general Marian continued to attend leftist anti-fascist meetings. Seeing the coming troubles he traveled for a month in search of a safe place that was cheap and remote; a warm refuge for a young family. He was unable to persuade his pregnant wife to move to an obscure part of Portugal with their two kids so they bought buy tickets for passage on a boat to Southampton. A week after their departure the Canary ports were closed and the headlines that greeted them in Britain told of the outbreak of the Spanish Civil War. Three months later the Jarrow March would pass through London, as would other anti-fascist and unemployed groups—people from his own country, unemployed miners, steelworkers, shipbuilders; hungry, angry people. But London put no bread in their mouths nor provided refuge for Bunting either because he had burnt his metropolitan literary bridges years before, when he wrote for an Italian newspaper in 1933 of the Bloomsbury crowd as "that dung heap believed to be a bed of lilies . . . the sweet, drippy, unbearable smell of decadence which has recently pervaded every English product . . . the stubborn rear-guard of a golden age in which the servants were servile and even the well-off tradesmen prudently bowed to Birth and Education." In 1932 he had also made a powerful enemy of T.S. Eliot when, in an issue of *Poetry* (Chicago), he criticized the older poet's magazine, *The Criterion*, which he called an "international disaster" since Elliot began to "love his gloom, and regretfully, resignedly, to set about perpetuating the causes of it—kings, religion and formalism . . . I have nothing to say against his poetry, amongst the finest of the age; but against his influence on the poetry of others, the involuntary extinguisher he applies to every little light, while professing, maybe truly, to hate the dark."

A much lesser, but influential, metropolitan force, Malcolm Muggeridge, was ridiculed in another review: "it is agreeable to fancy that some day it may not pay a man who has material for an essay to swell it to the length of a half guinea book by verbose repetition and argument round and round . . .' In 1972 after an appearance on TV I happened to come under the glare of Mr. Muggeridge. Muggeridge was then a governor of the BBC and said, in the hearing of the producer Barry Hanson, "that man will not work in the BBC again." Muggeridge, it was later revealed, was the British Intelligence conduit through which Stephen Spender's wages were paid when he was editor of the CIA house journal, *Encounter*. My TV performance also excited the distaste of the rightwing media watchdog and blacklist compilers, Aims of Industry.

"We're sending you to Poland, Pickard," Jeff Nuttall told me in the Spring of 1976. We were part of the rabble pack of 'entryist' poets democratically elected onto the committee of the National Poetry Society who'd recently made Eric Mottram editor of Poetry Review and Hugh MacDiarmid president. An invitation had come to Nuttall, as chairman, to send representatives to the International Poetry Festival, Warszawa Jesien, from the Polish Writer's Union. At the first railway stop in Holland I saw a Polish "Kontessa' struggling to get four heavy suitcases onto the train and got out to give her a hand. It took two of us to lift each case. After talking for a while I invited her to a sleeping car birth in the Russian carriage that I had managed to obtain for a few dollars, the best part of a bottle of whisky and a few salutations to international brotherhood. A wee spat blew up between the Kontessa and the Russian but when he left

13

us alone I muff-dived across the Iron Curtain—or the Spam Curtain as Alan Hull, songwriter from the band Lindisfarne, re-named it when I recounted the journey some years later. As the train entered and exited Berlin armed soldiers came in with dogs, stepladders and screw drivers in their search for illicit people or goods. Despite the discomfort of the thirty-six hour journey the high black-market exchange rate for the dollar in Poland would make it a cheap place to live—even for me.

When I stepped, hung-over, down onto the lonely Warsaw platform that ran along the line going straight through to Moscow there was a red banner draped over a fence that read "Welcome Comrade Delegates." At first I thought it was for the poets until the train disgorged a group of trade unionists, equally hung-over.

The value of living in a cheap place was laid bare to me when I was on remand in HMP Brixton a few months later, taking advantage of an hour out of the cell to exercise in the small, well-scuffed yard. Remand prisoners were, perhaps still are, banged up for twenty-three hours a day in very small cells built for one but accommodating three. They must also share the air with the three pots of their own excrement between infrequent slop outs—and take their meals where there is barely space for one person to stand between the bunks. While walking in circles around the exercise yard with Costos, a Greek Cypriot and one of my fellow accused, he asked where I would go to when I got out.

"Warsaw."

Costos was a dab hand at the three-card trick, which is performed on the run in Piccadilly and other heavily populated tourist spots.

"You should go to Uganda, my friend, you make good money."

"How?"

"You're a writer, aren't you?"

"Yeah, but . . ."

"You can make a lot of money."

"How?"

"Sell them biros."

"Don't take the piss," I told him, but he wasn't.

"Look, what I walk in, you can do it. See this suit?" he said, holding his arms wide to display it's cut, "I could sell this for £500. And these shoes," we both looked down at his smart foot-wear. "I get £300."

When the military dictator General Idi Amin threw the Asians and Europeans out of Uganda he lost a large swath of the merchant class and created a shortage of luxury Western goods for those who could afford and craved them. And Costos, as an exile in London, had served an apprenticeship to a fellow expat cobbler, so he knew shoes.

"What do you think I'd get?" He stopped and looked me over, tilting his head to one side and curling his mouth in appraisal.

"Well, maybe . . ." he began and paused empathetically.

"£20 for your suit. And your shoes..." his shoulders contracted and his voice became mater-of-fact again—"A fiver."

"Got a hole in my shoes, but am back on ma feet again." I sang a line from the old blues song. He smiled to himself and then walked in silent mediation.

"But, Lebanon!" He became soulful, "you could get anything in Beirut."

When we were being interrogated by the undercover Customs and Excise officers he kept silent and gave them his name, age and address only, until they coaxed a response from him, asking what he did for a living.

"General dealer."

"General Amin dealer?"

During the interrogations, which lasted from midnight to six the following evening, I remained silent or claimed bad memory, especially when confronted with the photographs they'd taken in which I wore that white cotton cap.

The raid on my flat took place two hours after a phone call to Joanna in Warsaw telling her that I had fixed up our next and (second) meeting—a holiday in Budapest at the Astoria Hotel. My passport was in the Hungarian Embassy being issued with a visa and I had paid the deposit on a 7-day trip to Budapest—£90 inclusive of room and food. Blissfully lit a spliff and settled down to work. I was beginning to see connections and gave the title "Détente" to a poem that I was working on.

a swallow flew into this room and banged against
      the window
I caught her in my hand and felt her heart pelt
      against my palm like rain
we were both held
her wide swift wings in my anxious grasp

I wish to tell you about my prison
my fingers are the wings of god
his crushing love rushes through their veins

o   o   o

After an hour's work on the poem I lit another spliff
and headed for the bog. There is no light bulb there as
it might reveal to any chance visitors peering through
the letterbox that I was home. Most chance visitors
tend to be bailiffs. Or perhaps it was a habit from my
childhood when my mother would hide behind the
sofa until the priest who was rattling at the letterbox
had given up and gone away in search of other sinners
with a glass or two of whisky as he put their wavering
world in order. Just as I unzipped my strides I heard
an urgent knocking and froze. Another loud knock.
They'll get sick before I do. Then a Newcastle voice
called through the letterbox.

"Tommy" The voice was intimate.

"Tommy" And familiar too. Hardly anyone calls
me Tommy, except those who have known me from
childhood. The voice was familiar, conspiratorial.

"Tommy, man" And urgent.

"Whose that?" I stupidly asked, breaking my
silence.

"Peter"

I knew a couple of Geordie Peters, both of whom
were capable of showing up late, looking for a doss.
"Peter who?"

"Peter Byker" Peter from Byker? Knowing at least one Peter from Byker I opened the door and six hefty guys stormed into the narrow corridor, two of then armed, and pinned me to the wall.

"You're bust, bonny lad."

One hour later two officers led me downstairs in handcuffs into the dark street where we got into an unmarked car which was driven to New Fetter Lane, near Fleet Street, and parked outside of an anonymous 1950s office block with no name plate on the door nor any indication of the nature of the business transacted there. I was taken into an empty office, on the fifteenth floor, with only a table and three chairs and which overlooked the Daily Mirror building. The two officials sat at an empty table and I was instructed to sit opposite. They studied me carefully as they loaded various files onto the desk between us. The senior officer opened an envelope and took out my slim month-at-a-glance diary for 1976 that had been removed in the raid.

"We've been following your career with great interest." He folded open the month of August.

"Are you a socialist?"

"I hope so. Why?"

"It says here, 'Picket South Africa House.' Did you organise the picket line?"

"No."

"What do you write poems about?"

"You didn't bring me here for a tutorial."

"You've really disappointed me. I used to be a fan of yours," said the Geordie arresting officer.

Did I let the team down? Is there a team? And if there was, would he and I be on the same one? His disappointment raised more questions than I had answers to. I had been on the periphery of a scam from which I had gained enough to send something North for the kids and something for my mother with enough left over to buy myself a drink—but I wasn't going to splurt mea culpa into his coffee cup. Had I let him down? And who was he anyway? And what precisely was it that he knew about me that brought us to this place, face-to-face at 2:35 AM?

His partner flipped open a file and produced a black and white photograph of Jack and me unloading a Ford Transit van in a street near Victoria, clearly shaking large plastic sheeting which, they suggested, was covered in traces of cannabis. We had been under surveillance for at least three months.

"That's you, isn't it?"

"I don't know." I was shocked.

"Why not?"

"I've never seen myself from behind before."

"You recognise the cap, though?"

He produced another photograph from the same occasion but on this one I was wearing a white cotton cap.

"It's the same cap as this, isn't it?" He showed me a press cutting from *Time Out* magazine that included a photograph of me wearing the same cap at a tilt—"Jack the Lad" having a laugh over an afternoon pint in an Irish bar in Northwest London. The article was about winning a C.D. Lewis Fellowship that situated me one day a week in a North London school for a couple of terms. It also mentioned that I was researching the Jarrow March in the Public Record Office where I was following a lead about a pre-war fascist conspiracy amongst leading industrialists and members of the establishment whose machinations had icily screwed and starved the Jarrow people. The BBC had been persuaded to partially commission a documentary for BBC

Third Programme, which meant that I could talk to and record survivors and witnesses of the 1936 "hunger march." It was an event known to me from an early age and I needed to find and lay out what I could of it. The Jarrow March was emblematic—regular Geordie issue baggage— an event that located the Northeast in the 1930s depression, despite the efforts of the new embarrassed image overlords. But it was also heroic and imbued with solidarity.

"Can you explain what you were doing on the occasion when these photographs were taken?"

They gave me the dates and times. I did not have the gall to plead my innocence and neither did I want to implicate anyone else so fell back on the felon's litany of dim recall. Another member of the "gang," an Irishman, who was being interviewed in another room, when confronted with the same volume of evidence held his hands up and admitted everything—but would say nothing about anyone else, fearing, he implied, retribution.

"Listen they are heavy people. They're bad news." When shown my photograph he said, "forget him." But I knew nothing of that then, sitting in the stark room being watched through a dark glass by a senior officer who came in during the integration and ordered me to sit down again when I got up to pace the floor. They had photographs. They had the ounce of grass from my desk, other officers were still searching my flat and perhaps they had found or would find the two kilos of grass, three thousand pounds, and a handgun that I'd concealed. One kilo of grass was mine but the money and the gun belonged to a friend.

The gun. Where had it been? What had it done? Of all the grass induced terrors that I suffered during the eighteen hours of arrest and interrogation the worst was the fear that they'd find the stash with the weapon. The interviews went on through the night, hour after hour, and I continued to plead bad memory or suggested an innocent explanation for the apparently damming evidence placed in front of me, but dread opened a chasm whenever I thought of the undiscovered gun. As the first team of interrogators changed over and the new ones came in my terror deepened—have they found the stash? The new team produced Jack's bank statements.

"Why has Jack been cashing cheques for you?"

"I'm overdrawn."

As an expression of his disapproval of my unruly life the Geordie officer shook his head.

"I bought your last book."

"That must have been the year my royalties doubled."

"Look Tom, I know you probably did this to raise money for a literary project."

They had clearly tapped into and sat through endless paranoid feuding literary telephone calls between me and the other plotters at the National Poetry Society in our head-on collision with the Arts Council, principal funding agency of the raggedy institution.

The C.D. Lewis Fellowship required me to "teach" one day a week in a London secondary school which subjected a few pupils suffering from wayward talent or a sense of withdrawal to long sessions with me. One of the kids, who later became a DJ for a London radio station, had written a long novel at the age of twelve, and with some of the other kids we invented the reggae haiku. A small Caribbean boy who remained mostly silent throughout the sessions—and who may have been sent into my room because his teachers didn't know what to do with him— handed me a handwritten poem the day before my arrest and I've kept it with me as a talisman ever since.

> I am cool ok
> and so tall ok
> I have free
> so they
> and you are so
> ugly no one
> can look at you

That was in November 1976, seven weeks after my return from Warsaw where I'd met and fallen in love with Joanna. By this time I was desperately trying to find the means to get back there or to bring her to London. Getting a passport from their government to travel to the West was as difficult for Polish citizens as it was for them to get an entry visa into Western countries. I was working, between long periods on the dole, in a range of poorly paid jobs none of which lasted more than a few weeks and was finding it difficult to pay the rent for the flat that I was illegally subletting from a friend of the poet and lyricist,

Pete Brown. Pete had helped me out once before, at the Edinburgh festival in 1965. While I was on stage at the Travers Theatre with a few fucked-off musicians from Newcastle, a theatre worker beckoned me off stage and told me that a couple of men wanted to see me and they wouldn't wait for the gig to finish.

"Who are they?"

"They don't look like poetry fans."

"Is there another way out of here?"

"Not really."

The men were thick-set and heavy shouldered.

"Mr. Pickard?"

"What wants to know?"

"Will you step outside for a moment, so we can talk?"

I followed them down the winding stairwell and when we got to a landing they snapped handcuffs on my wrists.

"The Newcastle police have a warrant for your arrest. They told us you'd be here."

There had been an article in the *Newcastle Journal* a week prior saying something like "Local Poet to Perform at Edinburgh Festival" and they must have added it to their clippings library.

"We're taking you back to Newcastle."

The charge was for an unpaid electricity bill that magistrates had upgraded to a civil debt, which meant imprisonment for nonpayment. As they led me down the stairs we passed Pete Brown.

"What's happening, man?"

"Pete, can you lend me a few quid?"

He had recently received an advance for lyrics that he was writing with Jack Bruce and Cream, and generously paid the police while I resumed my performance on stage, a little shaken.

The political atmosphere was tense at the time of the 1976 Warsaw "September Festival." A few months prior, striking shipyard workers in Gdánsk and Schezczin had been killed during a demonstration while others were imprisoned along with many supporters from the intelligencia including the then Trotskyist, Jacek Kuron, who later became a minister in the late 80s after the Solidarity revolution. Some of the Polish writers were very nervous and reticent to speak of the situation in the confined space of the Writer's Union restaurant but opened up as we wandered through the city. Walking up Nowy Swiat with an American writer who told me that he'd been asked by *Encounter* magazine to "see what you can get out of them," our Polish companion gave an account of the overt and covert lives that they were forced to lead. As he described the Samizdat system of underground publishing and the complexities of Stalinist censorship—how they employed scholars to interpret metaphors—the American adjusted a partially concealed microphone. When I asked our guide if he were aware of it his response was a mixture of fear and frozen fury.

"Your cassette could be confiscated at the border. I would be arrested." The American looked sheepish and put the kit away but I saw him trying again before we'd walked another ten yards. The foreign poets at the Warsaw festival were granted a five-day visa and five nights accommodation in Hotel Polonia, which we shared with a visiting symphony orchestra. This presented me with a problem, as I wanted to stay indefinitely to pursue my courting.

Earlier that year, back in London, I had gotten a job as a driver for a delicatessen merchant who supplied the boardroom kitchens of City institutions with their culinary needs (prunes on order every day) but after two weeks decided that I was being over-worked and underpaid—no overtime rates for instance—so called in one morning and tried to renegotiate my salary. As labour was cheap and plentiful they sacked me.

> when these gentlemen
> eat their prunes and shit
> the pound will float
> and we will swim in it

Jack met me later in the day for a beer and said that he might be able to help out with a few days driving work—nothing he could talk about and in fact the less I knew the better it was for me. It wasn't wise to work blind, but I trusted him and needed the money. A couple of weeks later we hired a van and I drove him to a tool suppliers on the Tottingham Court Road where he purchased some very heavy bolt-cutters from a wry shop assistant who said, "Oh no, not another Geordie fucking safe-cracker." The following mid-day we drove to South London and parked the van outside of a pub and went in for a drink. Jack left quickly telling me to stay-put until he came back. He'd not gone long when Spud appeared red-eyed and flushed.

"How's it gannin?" I asked him. He presumed that I knew everything.

"It's fucking unbelievable, Tommy, man. There must be near a ton of grass. I hope there's no fucking bodies in the boxes, though."

"Where they from?"

"Uganda."

He was sweating and joyful from unpacking the crates. The news was a relief to me—it's only grass—but sparked a thread of fear at the scale of it. Caught up in the middle of the enterprise I couldn't see a way out but was cheered at the prospect of a decent bung. When Jack came back I told him what I knew and he was pissed off as it was his intention to keep me uninformed for my protection and his profit, I suppose.

We drove up a narrow cut and parked the van outside of an ordinary semi-detached house, whose owners were on holiday. There was a lawn out back overlooked by French windows and over the fence in an adjoining garden a woman hung her washing on a line to dry. It was a warm summer's day and children played in the street. In the spacious living room I helped to open several large sealed wooden crates so the Greeks could check and weigh their contents: almost one ton of Ugandan bush which had been taken out of a bonded warehouse at the airport where it was officially awaiting transhipment. A little of the bush had to be stored overnight in my flat while the rest remained crated in the van parked outside. We filled a deep bathtub to the taps and when they left I skimmed off a kilo for a bonus, suspecting that my wages would not be commensurate with the risk I was taking. Fearing to conclude their business in the dark in case it drew attention, the armed Greeks insisted on staying at Jack's basement flat and treated him as surety until they could collect their share the following day. They drank whisky and played cards all night. Then the crates had to be emptied and refilled with ballast and returned to the bonded warehouse to conclude the transhipment.

At first they were to be filled with hand carved African dolls but the dispatchers of the crates in Uganda had declared the contents on the Customs form as "personal goods." The dolls were thought too incongruous to serve that description so I suggested books and sold them all the volumes I had of *Strand Magazine* (which weighed in at ten kilos), an incomplete set of *Encyclopaedia Britannica* 9th edition, and a set of *The Times History of World War I*. Seeing all that ballast removed from my own shelves lifted my spirit. I thought I'd never get rid of them. However it was nowhere near enough so we drove the wagon to a second-hand bookshop in Marylebone, where we purchased three dozen cloth bound volumes of *Punch* and ten cloth bound volumes of *Boys Own*. We were the kind of customer that I could only dream about in my book dealing days. The shop was inadequately stocked with heavy volumes so we drove to Farringdon Road where we purchased from the stalls set out there another two sets of *The Times History of World War I*, along with some religious authors. I sniffed amongst the books while Jack sat in the back of the wagon with the scales calculating the weight of the library that we were acquiring.

"We need another 250 kilo," he told me.

The ancient bookseller was blissful as we bought much of his space wasting dust gathering, back breaking, spirit deadening unread and unreadable religious and military texts; all those pounds of printed pages by puffing parsons, anaemic academics, bloated bishops, geriatric generals, corpulent combatants and high ranking haemorrhoidal heroes. All that catechistic cataplasm, that militarist mucus, that pedantic pus from festering farts. The engaging entrails of emetic ambassadors, pestiferous papers by prudish pedagogues. I struggled to the wagon with arms full of books, and still he wasn't satisfied—so I purchased conquering chronicles by conceited commanders, acned abortions by abstemious abstractors, asphyxiating articles by arthritic archbishops, bromidicidal broadsides by bumptious broadcasters, asthmatic excretions by abject aesthetes, moralising morsels from mealy mouthed manufacturers, windy waffle from former centre forwards, bird brained banter by juiced-up journos, celebrity cackle from coked-up cacky-crammed crack heeds, pontificating prime-time poseurs promoting puffed-up personalities, mendacious manuals by manic muff munching mullahs, post-modern pancakes flipped from non-stick pans stuck to the threadbare ceiling of their own gravity defying gravitas. And it still wasn't enough so I bought the works of talk show hosts, canting sofa cunts coughing up chintzy chunder, bloated volumes by toady poets who sit in circles blowing prizes up each others arseholes with straws—until we'd filled the crates.

I thought nothing else about it until I was arrested and remanded in HMP Brixton three months later when a Customs & Excise squad caught my friend and his colleagues with a second shipment that I had no knowledge of nor involvement with. They had been informed of the first transaction and had begun a stake out when we were loading the van and followed us as the crime proceeded. But I somehow, and unknowingly, made a wrong turn into an apparent cu-de-sac- and managed to lose the convoy of police and customs' vehicles that were tailing and ahead of us. To recover their position they decided to mount surveillance, and for the next three months the phones were tapped and we were followed. Picking up the telephone one day I heard the security at Heathrow airport informing an operative that George Harrison and his wife were travelling under the names of Mr. and Mrs. Smith on flight 251 to New York.

Although it deepened a suspicion that the phone was tapped I attributed that to my relentless traffic in love letters across the Iron Curtain as well as the research I was doing into an element of the British ruling class collaborating with Nazi Germany and a "conspiracy" associated with the Jarrow March. However, it was between the first importation from Uganda and the second that I made the trip to Poland, fell in love and was desperate to go back. By the time I came to leave Warsaw we'd learnt enough of each other's worlds and words to want to meet again, but perhaps in another country, one that we could both visit without too much bureaucratic hassle. We decided on Budapest because it was a city that neither of us had been to. I would try to raise the money for the trip by selling the kilo of grass that I'd skimmed. A journey across the divide—Churchill's *Iron Curtain* or Alan Hull's *spam curtain*—a new intriguing girl with her own gaff and a new cheap city—what a vision to hold in mind. Somehow I was able to blag the soldiers on the train with sign language when they noticed that my visa had over-run by 10 days—or maybe they didn't care—and I began the thirty-six hour train journey back to

London, with a packed lunch and her scented scarf to keep me warm. I shared the compartment with an old peasant man without a word in common. We sat opposite each other at the window seats and gazed at the land as we glided over it. Long before dusk a deep mist rose over the woodlands and the landscape of thin strip farming. He opened his bait box and took out an apple, slicing off thin slivers with a knife that looked as old and knarred as the hands that held it, offering me a slice or two balanced on the blade.

When I got home to my flat in London the electricity and gas had been cut off for non-payment and I went to bed cold and angry. Next day I awoke aching from the train journey but visited the Hungarian Embassy to apply for a visa. By the following week I had sold enough grass to send money north for the kids, pay the rent and the get the electricity turned back on. One month later I purchased an airline ticket and booked a room in the old Hotel Astoria. Jack and his colleagues made the second transhipment five days before I was due to meet Joanna in Hungary. This time customs and police were following them all the way, and after a car chase they were arrested. Within the hour they came for me.

After my interrogation in Fetter Lane and on the way to the police station where we were to be held for a second night and charged I asked the customs officers if I could stop at a newsagents to buy a copy of *The Listener* as I wanted to read a review of my radio documentary about the Jarrow March broadcast the week before. They generously agreed, uncuffed me and I went to make the purchase. The review was niggardly, and in those circumstances it flattened me and I felt hopeless and worthless. When we arrived at the police station, Jack and I were charged and locked up in separate cells. These were modern, windowless, and overheated and I wondered about the architect who had designed them. It was the first time that I'd been alone in almost twenty hours and I felt dirty and dehydrated. I could see Jack through the spy hole in the opposite cell walking back and forth, but could not catch his attention. I lay down and fell asleep only to be woken half an hour later by the desk sergeant who flung open the hatch.

"Are you hungry?"

"Fuckin clammin, marra."

"Breakfast at eight, then." He slammed the hatch shut and I fell asleep again.

Somehow I was able to disconnect my erect cock and she began to suck it like a lollipop but without excitement. How can I reconnect it? Would I stitch it? Although there was no thrill in the member my groin ached with desire. A young girl, with whom I was infatuated, turned her head towards me with an inviting look.

"I was wondering how long your youth would last," she said.

"Why don't you live with me for three or four years and find out?"

"That's too long. I'll give you one. Or two, perhaps."

We passed the dark windows of an empty house with mouldy curtains that were crumbling like Mrs. Haversham's wedding dress.

"We can live in there," she said as we went into a shadow-deep room with three unmade mouldy beds over which we had to walk. Stepping from the first bed

to the second my foot sunk into what was clearly an
unresponsive body concealed beneath dirty bedding.

"There's someone in here and they're dead."

The girl peeled away the sheeting, which fell apart
in her hand and cried out when she saw an old wom-
an's corpse, which I was afraid to look at. I drew the
girl's warm body close for her comfort and for mine.

And woke from the dream of love sex and death.
Cold. The electric light was burning out of reach
and my nostrils were baked and hurt. The cell,
lined with modern white tiles and studiously
inhuman, was almost airtight and stunk pain-
fully of an excess of disinfectant. The brown
paint on the door was scraped and inscribed with
names and a street in Belfast. There was no way
of knowing what time it was or for how long
I had slept and my throat was sore with refus-
ing to answer questions. Next morning we were
taken to the magistrates court, denied bail, and
remanded to Brixton prison. We were loaded
onto a meat wagon and shut in locker sized cubi-
cles that were so narrow my knees touched the
walls opposite when seated. Jack told me later
that he grabbed a quick one off the wrist in his

cubicle on the journey from courtroom to jail because it would be a long while before he'd have the privacy to do it again. As we travelled through the streets of London from courtroom to jail I wondered how long it would be before I'd see my family again and how to get a letter to Warsaw in time to warn Joanna that I couldn't make Budapest.

I sat with eight other men who had come from court in the draughty reception room with benches along the walls. At one end a prison officer stood at a high desk filling in forms. The prisoners shared tobacco—and sought a supply of matches. He faced the official in a half dream, then became aware of an aggravated impatience.

"Have you been in prison before?"

"No."

"Got to start some time. What religion are you?"

"Pantheist."

"We'll put you down as 'nil'. Sit down and wait till you hear your name."

"Next" An old man got up. One eye was blackened and blood-shot, his mouth was caked black with dried blood and clear liquid ran from his nose. The corridor

was long and bleak and cold. The place was Dickensian, gothic, disgusting. Not an atheist. Nil. Short for Nihilist, maybe.

When my name was called out I went into a room with another pulpit-like desk around which several guards stood. They directed me to a set of large scales and told me to undress. Naked, I stepped onto the scales and my weight was recorded in a ledger. A guard with a white coat over his uniform dropped my balls into the palm of his hand and told me to cough. They directed me to a counter from which an officer distributed a towel, a bar of soap and a razor and pointed me towards the bath. Hot clean water. It was the first time that I'd been able to wash the stink of fear from my body in twenty-four hours and I relaxed momentarily. After getting dressed we were taken to C wing and stood in a queue on the ground floor next to some small cells. I was ushered into one where a hearty robust woman in late middle-age greeted me and introduced her sidekick, a mild mannered and thin man in his late fifties whom she would not allow to speak. She was a Shavian character, hungry for souls.

"*I see you've entered 'nil' for religion but I thought I'd have you in for a chat. We're C of E so they usually* send us the atheists. Now, the first thing I tell prisoners when they come in is that I've got nothing to do with the prison. Anything that you say in here is absolutely confidential and doesn't leave these four walls. So, if you've anything to get off your chest . . . you are down here as no religion but sometimes a little chat helps."

"I'm a pantheist."

"A what?"

"He means a nature worshiper . . . and they believe that . . ." her companion failed to complete his sentence.

"Why were you arrested?"

"I'm accused of smuggling cannabis into the country."

"And did you?"

"No."

"Are you with those other people, standing outside?"

"Yes."

"And did they do it?"

"No."

She looked at me carefully.

"Do you take drugs?"

"A bit of smoke."

"What a world this is turning into."

o o o

After the inductions we were allocated cells. Spud Murphy and I shared one with a young cockney thief—or so he said. Such was our paranoia that we suspected he may have been planted with us, which meant that we couldn't talk openly in front of him. I chose the high bunk and Spud the one beneath and the cockney the one opposite. I thought the higher bunk would provide more privacy, or maybe it was a regression to childhood and the delight of riding on the top deck of buses. But it was a mistake as I found later. Most people in a remand prison who intend to plead innocent are rehearsing their defence from the moment of induction and live in a permanent state of fear and uncertainty until the outcome of the trial. The place stinks of fear and stink rises; the top bunk was not a wise choice. As soon as we were settled the young cockney made a request.

"Look, try not to shit in the pots cos we'll be smelling it all night. If you can, wait till slop out in the morning." But on that first night my guts gave out. All that fear and bad food conflated into an explosion. Likewise Spud. We were apologetic but the cockney shrugged it off.

"We'll try and get some newspapers or paper

bags tomorrow and make shit parcels if it 'appens agin," he explained. What that meant was we could shit in a newspaper or paper bag and throw it out of the window into the yard where it would be collected next day by someone on shit parcel duty. But at least we wouldn't have to sleep with the stink in our nostrils all night. Unable to talk freely to Spud and exhausted from the endless interrogations I just wanted to lie down and sleep. When the lights in the cells went out the cockney lay on his bunk and looked at the door with the light from the corridor visible through the spy hole.

"Just think of it as the moon shining through a forest." His words were the last I heard before falling into an exhausted sleep where I dreamt that I fathered a child and witnessed its birth. As soon as he was born the child began to speak fluently and eloquently; I felt joyful. Then I was riding a horse with Joanna over steep hills above San Francisco looking at the ancient walls of China. We rode through generous, spacious country until a bell rang and the cell door was flung open. A wretched, shrivelled man stood snivelling over the pots of strong tea that he

49

poured us from a large aluminium teapot carried on a trolley as he regurgitated the circumstances of his arrest and rehearsed his defence as though he'd known us all his life. And it was clear that he did this in most cells on the wing.

"What do you think of me chances?" he asked, after a long explanation of the circumstances that led to his arrest.

"You'll walk it," I told him.

"Yeah, the fucking plank," Spud added.

We drank the tea and rolled a smoke.

"Have you got some matches?" the cockney asked me so I threw him what I had and he took out the blade from his razor and began to carefully and slowly slice each match into two sometimes three flares that would light a snout. A screw came by and told us "slop out" and we picked up our pots, formed a line and followed through to the bathroom where we dumped our crap and washed up. There was a short row of toilets with sawn-off doors, up-lifted by a few steps from the floor. This is what you were meant to hold out for. The throne of shyte. After the slop-out we went downstairs through the cage for breakfast.

o   o   o

Living in London without the means to travel back to see the kids often enough was corrosive. I could have remained in Gateshead, a few streets away, but my life had fallen apart then too when I could find no work of any kind to pay the bills. But I knew that the kids knew who we were and where we were, and where we are still. And that's all there is to say about it.

There was no work in Newcastle worth the money until Eddy Kelley said he could get me started labouring on the city centre redevelopment. It was the highest paid building site in the city but it was against my principles because they were knocking the bollix out of the old "toon" about which I had recently shot my mouth off on a BBC TV arts program and got onto the Aims of Industry blacklist.

"Our new Bias prize, the Bent Microphone award, goes to *Full House*, a BBC2 programme on December 9 centred on Newcastle. Bias Prize for this month goes to this programme, in which Newcastle was taken as the theme. Words by

Tom Pickard, poet, refer to the speculative boot being put into Newcastle. The poem by Pickard called "Guttersnipe" was read by him, This portrayed the views and values of a factory manager who believed the poet should be a labourer to breathe the fumes of capital. Industry is love, industry is life. Allusion made to the poet's father who died from the fumes and factory work—supposedly nobly, from the manager's view. This was the real dark satanic mills stuff that Dickens might have scripted if he had been alive.*"

But the rent was in arrears and it was too late to stop the rapist redevelopment so I accepted Eddie's offer and agreed to meet early Monday morning when he would introduce me to the chippy foreman. Just as I turned up at the building site to start work the lads came out on strike and there was nowt else to do but join the picket line. The company brought in train loads of scabs from London and after six weeks I despaired walking one night back over the new Redheaugh

*Aims of Industry bulletin no. 6 Report On Industry On Television

bridge across the black Tyne to Gateshead with the traffic roaring past and a fierce wind raging. I just screamed from the lining of me guts into the gale. The next morning I threw some clothes and books together in preparation for a gig at Ted Hughes's Arvon Foundation in Devon where I was booked to spend the week as an instructor for a bunch of would-be writers, setting them exercises and reading over their creations. It was the only "honest" money I would earn that summer, if money can ever be said to be "honest." As I found my seat and looked back across the Tyne to Newcastle the train gathered speed and I knew that I wouldn't be coming back. I was joining the region's oldest growth industry— the drift South—and resented it and the pain of leaving the kids.

Before breakfast anyone who wanted to see the doctor gave in their name and cell number. I'd woken with a raw throat, no doubt caused by the eighteen hours of interrogation I'd undergone the day before and the airless disinfectant police cell. The doctor looked into my throat and suggested I gargle with salty water. But the good news was that remand prisoners were allowed to have food and half a bottle of wine a day brought in. When I was told that I had a visitor my spirit lifted. My good friend Eric Mottram was waiting in the visitors room and I went to sit opposite, disturbed to see him mopping his eyes. Although distressed by my dilemma his tears were for his dying mother. I assured him that I was okay, in good company, and there wasn't much else to say, really, because it looked as though I was fucked. He'd brought me a half bottle of wine and some decent food, and a book that he thought I ought to read, he insisted, with care; Joseph Conrad's *Under Western Eyes*. When I returned to the cell I found that my fellow inmates had been blessed with visitors who had brought the small allowance of alcohol. We drank our own that day but agreed for the future that one of us would drink all three portions every three days and get drunk. When it was the cockney's turn to get pissed he spoke a poem from memory that he'd composed on a previous stay about how the cell's narrow walls had seen so much and so many.

After a time on remand in that shit-pit a compassionate friend, the TV and film producer, Barry Hanson, managed to raise the enormous bail by persuading a dozen writers of his acquaintance to pool in for half of it while the mercurial accountant to the stars, Michael Henshaw, stood up for the rest. The conditions of my bail were to surrender my passport and sign on at the Edgware Road police station twice a day—which made any trip out of London impossible. After a while I'd sign my name in different coloured inks to relive the boredom. At Christmas the courts gave permission to visit my old mother and the kids back in Newcastle provided I sign-on twice a day at the police station there. My widowed mother was seventy-eight, living alone in her council house. She was in fact my maternal great aunt and had adopted me at the age of nine months and changed my name in the process from McKenna to Pickard. We sat at her hearth and I told her that I was in trouble, that I may go to jail, and that I was sorry to bring shame to her doorstep. She took it better than I thought and brightened up when I told her of Joanna in Warsaw.

"She's welcome here, tell her."

In the year leading up to the trial I sold off most of my possessions, including a first edition of Oscar Wilde's *Salome* with Beardsley illustrations and a few other treasures acquired over a decade of book dealing and scouring junk shops and out of the way auction rooms. My friend, the poet Ken Smith, made a badge, which said "Tom Pickard is almost innocent," which was quite accurate but grim comfort. The night before the trail a drunken friend gave herself to me but I was too pissed and strung out to fuck so she blew me on the spiral stone steps of my Regent's Park Nash squat. With a hangover I entered the Central Criminal Court to surrender my bail and was taken down into the holding cells to wait for the trial to begin. Jack and I were banged up there with a bunch of guys from the East End accused of gang warfare over ice-cream wagons in the West End. They were curious about the developing drug scene and offered me a job with them when I got out. We were called up into the court and I sat next to Costos whom I'd not seen since Brixton prison and he talked about Cyprus and why he could never return. He had fallen in love and made pregnant the daughter of a powerful boss and wanted to marry her. Walking in the hills one day they noticed a priest running towards them looking purposeful but dishevelled and when he pulled a gun Costos ran, dodging the bullets. He went into hiding for a week, took a boat to Turkey where, after a month or so got arrested but broke out of jail and escaped to England. There was another Greek Cypriot in the dock, too, whom Jack named after a comic book character, Torpedo Tony, because he was armed and edgy—with a bullet shaped head. When his barrister asked for a Greek interpreter the judge agreed saying, "Are we going to need one for the Geordies?" Joanna managed to get a short visa and came to stay with me for the second week of the trial and I would try to keep her entertained by getting a guard to pass notes, which he did until ordered to cease. The notes said "see you in BUDAPEST!" or just "BUDAPEST." It's difficult to maintain a courtship from the dock. The prosecutor had a thin hatchet face and whenever my name was mentioned from the witness box he would turn to look at me with a sallow grin. On the morning of my cross examination we all stood in the corridor outside of the court room waiting for the doors to be opened, when the prosecutor entered wearing wig and gown. As he approached he smiled and spoke directly, with deliberate and considered courtesy, to me.

"Good morning," as though I were the morsel he was to have for breakfast.

Before my brain could catch up with my mouth I replied with equal courtesy. "Good morning. Have you been sharpening your teeth all night?"

His cross-examination was conducted with icy vigour. My hopeless defence was based on ignorance of the crime. It was such a shaky base that my legs weakened and I asked the judge if I could sit in the witness box, which he allowed.

The prosecutor presented apparently irrefutable evidence of my criminal involvement.

"Would you look at this photograph Mr. Pickard?" A copy of the same document was passed to the jury. It was an undercover picture of my friend and me removing boxes from a van outside of his basement flat in Victoria.

"Is that Mr. Blackburn?" the prosecutor asked me.

"It looks like him."

"And is that you helping him?"

"It could be."

"But you admit that you were packing boxes?"

"Yes, he bought a lot of books."

"Oh, you are a book dealer, are you?"

"Yes."

"I see. What books did your friend buy?"

"All sorts. Victorian a lot of them."

"Victorian? Such as?"

"Well, *The Strand Magazine*."

"That is not Victorian," the judge interrupted, "that is Edwardian. I used to read them as a lad and would not like to think of myself as a Victorian. *The Strand* was Georgian."

"Well," I spluttered, "they used to publish Rider Haggard, and he was a Victorian."

"Perhaps he was both," the judge continued, "and of course Conan Doyle—he also straddled the reigns of Victoria and George V."

The prosecutor patiently waited for the bench to finish.

"If you had known that your friend was importing large quantities of marijuana would you have informed the police?"

I appealed to the judge, complaining that it was a hypothetical question, but he insisted on an answer. This was the most difficult question so far, possibly because I hadn't seen it coming and couldn't see a way out of it—I was being invited to add a lie to the pile of half-truths that lay strewn at my feet. My friend was pleading guilty and was not in court. I hesitated—we were born in the same month of the same year and in the same street, we had been truants together, been in the same street gangs, taken our first illicit taste of alcohol and smoke together. Since moving to London he had fed me when I was skint, listened for long nights to my misery at being separated from the kids, kept me in drinks and smokes, and had given me a floor to sleep on in his cold damp basement flat that had been a hole in the wall for many Geordie friends on the run from the law. And when we were under arrest, during the long interrogation, the senior investigator said to me, "he'd trust you with his life, wouldn't he?" I had never thought of it before. To admit it would compound my guilt and confirm his suspicion of my involvement but I did not deny it. At the trial I replied to the prosecutor, "Yes, I'd report him if I'd known." My friend would understand but I felt terrible shame for saying it and could hardly look the jury in the eye. Some days before, during the prosecution case while a Customs officer was giving testimony, the judge was passed a note from the foreman of the jury who was I think, a Geordie chippy. The judge stopped the cross examination of the officer.

"I have been passed a note from the foreman of the jurors who asks, 'Why is the chief Custom's officer nodding and winking to the officer in the witness box?' I am sure that he is not acting improperly but I felt that I ought to air the concern of the jury and address it."

So the jury was clearly ready to listen with an open mind, and might even be inclined to give the benefit of the doubt. Sometimes when I reflect on the trial or recollect it for someone I catch myself referring to the jury as "the audience." Perhaps it was a performers instinct, but I knew that I had given the wrong answer and after what seemed a long while and following a further few penetrating and discomforting enquiries I interrupted the prosecutor.

"On reflection, and regarding an earlier question, I'd have to say that I wouldn't inform on my friend if I'd known he was smuggling dope." He scored many points after that and I thought my case lost but felt better for putting on the public record that I wasn't a grass. Perhaps that bit of honesty at least helped me out of the corner that the prosecutor had so easily boxed me into. At the end of my long cross examination, it lasted a day and a half, I shakily resumed my seat next to Costos while witnesses to my previous good character were drummed in. Amongst others, Eric Mottram and the film director, Lindsay Anderson spoke eloquently but the prosecutor ignored them until my final witness, Basil Bunting, took the witness stand. *Ex Wing Commander Bunting.* All that my friends could say was that I'd been honest in my dealings and that I was a decent poet, which, as the judge later pointed out in his summing up, bore no relevance to my guilt or innocence and reminded the jury of the 15th century French poet who was also a famous criminal.

"Who's that?" whispered Costos.

"Francois Villon. My mate translated him when he was in jail for being a conchy in the First World War."

> Mine was a three plank bed whereon
> I lay and cursed the weary sun.
> They took away the prison clothes
> and on the frosty nights I froze.
> I had a bible where I read
> that Jesus came to raise the dead—
> I kept myself from going mad
> by singing an old bawdy ballad

Bunting was seventy-seven years old and had served in the RAF and in Intelligence during World War II. He'd also temporally been a diplomat, a visiting professor, looked the world directly in the eye and had a dignified gait. The old poet had come from Northumberland to speak at the trial but he had written a series of letters during the year to prepare me for the worst. In response to my suggestion that I could use the imprisonment to do some writing, he responded with an account of his time in Windsor jail.

"If you get locked up I do not think they

would let you write,—this is not America. I know our gaols have been reformed, but not, I think, that much. 1918 all the writing even the most privileged were allowed to do was confined to a slate. When you had filled the slate you wiped it off and started again. Most of us didn't even have a slate. You were allowed to receive one letter and write one, as much as you could get onto one very small sheet of notepaper, every month after the first three, which were blank, provided you broke no rules meanwhile. You were allowed to talk, an hour a day, after the first two years, which were silent. No doubt all that has changed, but I do not think that it has been made what you and I would consider civilised. . . .but even now I know that you are not allowed to describe a prison or what goes on in it—no diary or description in letters – nor to take any writing out of prison until it has been passed by the authorities. You have to save it all up in your head. The difficulty would be to avoid becoming embittered, for rant about the hardship does no good at all and can narrow and cripple your own mind."

And in another letter he sought to encourage me.

"Hardship and humiliation, though severe, didn't give me any cause for despair. Yet I was a boy, eighteen, with nothing I could look back on to bolster my self-esteem or my courage. You have solid accomplishment to stiffen you . . . You can endure whatever they are likely to inflict on you, and it won't last for ever. It need not embitter you, let alone demolish you. Afterwards, freedom, with a deepened experience and perhaps a more accurate measure of yourself; and no less pride, though perhaps a less truculent pride."

Then a few days before the trail began a more rueful note.

"It may be that this is the last chance I'll have of addressing you before the verdict. What I chiefly want to say is that conviction and imprisonment would not be the end of your career by any means, nor would it alienate your friends. Prison is hard to bear, but it is not unbearable, and if you want to keep your eyes open to what is around you (as I'm pretty sure you will) you'll pile up a stock of experience you can make good use of in poetry eventually. Keep objective. Your own unhappiness is not capital stock, but what your eyes see and your ears hear is . . .

I quite expect neither to hear from you nor to be able to write to you if you are sentenced. You'll need your letters for more intimate folk, children, ex-wife, girl, etc. Bearing my age in mind, I may not be around if you are released after a long time; so let me say now that I have always admired your courage against odds, your readiness to learn whatever there was to learn, your goodwill even to people who have earned no good will; and I value your ear for rhythm, your readiness to cut down to what's essential, the way you evoke an emotion without a word that isn't concrete and factual."

Bunting was someone the jury clearly felt comfortable with, which may be why the prosecutor rose to ask a question just as the old gentleman picked up his walking stick and was about to be helped from the witness box.

"Wing Commander Bunting, would you still think so highly of Mr. Pickard if you knew that he took drugs?"

He smiled benignly and without a moment's hesitation replied. "I would be surprised if a man of his generation didn't."

As Bunting walked out of court Costos said, as much to himself as to those in earshot:

"What a fucking beautiful old man."

Jack and Spud pleaded guilty and were sentenced to eight years. There was a hung jury for Costos and he was committed to a retrial but he almost immediately skipped bail and the last I heard he'd been killed pulling a stroke. I was found not guilty by a majority verdict.

One week later Lindsay Anderson lent me the money to buy an airline ticket to Warsaw and we flew there together—he to show his films and lecture and I to meet the woman who had waited a year for my return. We cleared customs and immigration control and once out into the airport, a short taxi-ride from my lover and a long way from a year of sweated fear, I took a deep breath, opened my arms and said, with a touch of irony; "Ah, freedom."

"Dear boy," Lindsay chided, "you never know who's listening."

o   o   o

TOM PICKARD, and his then wife Connie, set up and curated the Mordern Tower poetry reading series in a near derelict tower on the medieval city walls of Newcastle upon Tyne in 1963 where Basil Bunting first read *Briggflatts* and Allen Ginsberg gave his first European performance of "Kaddish". For many years it was an essential international beacon for "counter culture" British and American poets.

He has published two books of oral/social history centered on shipbuilding and several book of poetry. There are four books currently in print, *fuckwind* Etruscan Books, and three, with Flood Editions, *Hole in The Wall (New and Selected Poems)*, *The Dark Months of May*, and, *Ballad of Jamie Allan* which was a National Book Critics' Circle Award finalist. *Ballad of Jamie Allan* is also a libretto for a folk opera composed by John Harle for whom Pickard has also written the words for a cantata for choir and saxophone, *Song For London Bridge*. It was premiered in Southwark Cathedral by Kings College Choir, Cambridge.

Pickard has lived in Poland and America where he often gives performances. He now resides on a foggy hill in the North Pennines.